TABLE OF CONTENTS

SMALL GROUP

The fact that you are even reading this page says a lot about you. It says that you are either one of those people that has to read everything, or you are at least open to being used by God to lead a group.

Leading a small group can sound intimidating, but it really doesn't have to be. Think of it more as gathering a few friends to get to know each other better and to have some discussion around spiritual matters.

Here are a few practical tips to help you get started:

1. PRAY

   One of the most important principles of spiritual leadership is to realize you can't do this on your own. No matter how long we've been leading, we need the power of the Holy Spirit. Lean on Him... He will help you.

2. INVITE SOME FRIENDS

   Don't be afraid to ask people to come to your group. You will be surprised how many people are open to such a study, especially when you let them know that the study is only for eight weeks. Whether you have 4 of 14 in your group, it can be a powerful experience. You should probably plan on at least an hour and a half for your group meeting.

3. GET YOUR MATERIALS

   You will need to get a DVD of the video teaching done by Chip Ingram. You can get the DVD from LivingontheEdge.org Also, it will be helpful for each person to have their own study guide. You can also purchase those through the website.

4. BE PREPARED TO FACILITATE

   Just a few minutes a week in preparation can make a huge difference in the group experience. Each week preview the video teaching and review the discussion questions. If you don't think your group can get through all the questions, select the ones that are most relevant to your group.

5. LOVE YOUR GROUP

   Maybe the most important thing you bring to the group is your personal care for them. If you will pray for them, encourage them, call them, e-mail them, involve them, and love them, God will be pleased and you will have a lot of fun along the way.

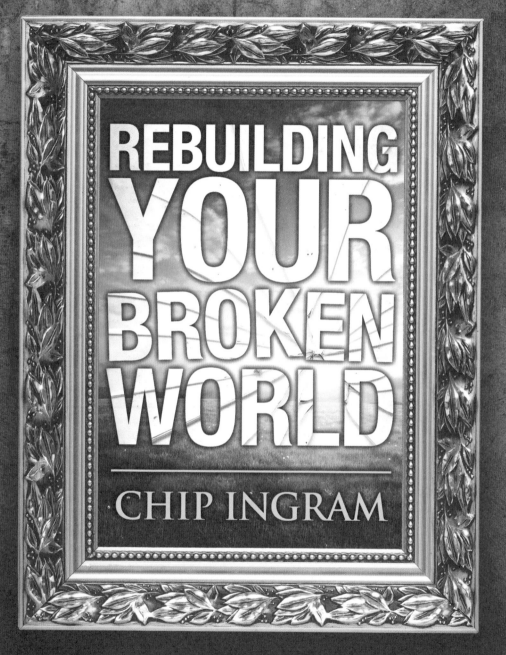

REBUILDING YOUR BROKEN WORLD

CHIP INGRAM

Rebuilding Your Broken World

EXPERIENCE

You and your group are about to begin what could be a life-changing journey in your small group. This practical series will help you and your group discover God's plan for handling life's challenges.

Listed below are the segments you will experience each week as well as some hints for getting the most out of this experience.

 TAKE IT IN: During this section you will watch the video teaching. Each teaching segment is about 25 minutes long. A teaching outline with fill-ins is provided for each session. As you follow along, write down questions or insights that you can share during the discussion time. Also, bring your Bible each week.

 TALK IT OVER: Several discussion questions are provided for your group to further engage the teaching content. Keep the following guidelines in mind for having a healthy group discussion.

- **Be involved.** Jump in and share your thoughts. Your ideas are important, and you have a perspective that is unique and can benefit the other group members.

- **Be a good listener.** Value what others are sharing. Seek to really understand the perspective of others in your group and don't be afraid to ask follow up questions.

- **Be courteous.** Always treat others with utmost respect. When there is disagreement, focus on the issue and never turn the discussion into a personal attack.

- **Be focused.** Stay on topic. Help the group explore the subject at hand, and try to save unrelated questions or stories for afterwards.

- **Be careful not to dominate.** Be aware of the amount of talking you are doing in proportion to the rest of the group, and make space for others to speak.

- **Be a learner.** Stay sensitive to what God might be wanting to teach you through the lesson, as well as through what others have to say.

 LIVE IT OUT: These simple suggestions help the lesson come to life. Don't ignore them; give them a try! Check in with another group member during the week and ask how it's going.

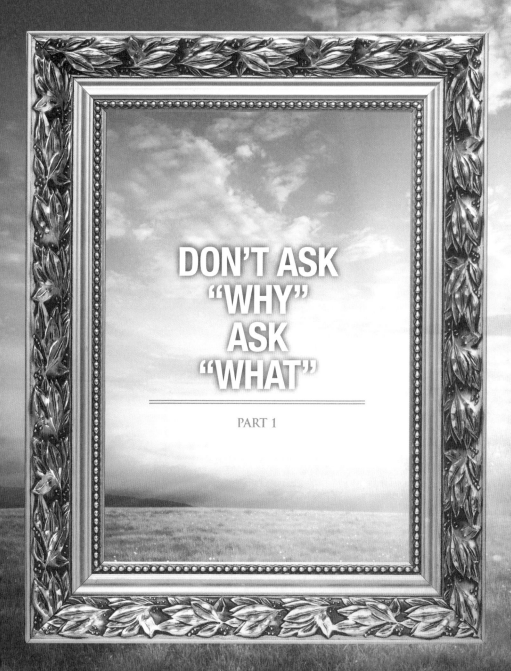

DON'T ASK "WHY" ASK "WHAT"

PART 1

SESSION 1

Everybody has _____ experiences.

We live in a fallen world and bad things happen to bad people. And bad things happen to good people.

THREE OBSERVATIONS ABOUT LIFE

1. Trials are _____.

    In a fallen world bad times are not a possibility, they are a promise.

DEAR FRIENDS, DO NOT BE SURPRISED AT THE FIERY ORDEAL THAT HAS COME ON TO TEST YOU, AS THOUGH SOMETHING STRANGE WERE HAPPENING TO YOU.

1 PETER 4:12 (NIV)

"THESE THINGS I HAVE SPOKEN TO YOU, THAT IN ME YOU MAY HAVE PEACE. IN THE WORLD YOU WILL HAVE TRIBULATION; BUT BE OF GOOD CHEER, I HAVE OVERCOME THE WORLD."

JOHN 16:33 (NKJV)

EVERYONE WHO WANTS TO LIVE A GODLY LIFE IN UNION WITH CHRIST JESUS WILL BE PERSECUTED; AND EVIL PERSONS AND IMPOSTORS WILL KEEP ON GOING FROM BAD TO WORSE, DECEIVING OTHERS AND BEING DECEIVED THEMSELVES.

2 TIMOTHY 3:12-13 (GN)

2.   Trials tend to make us or _____.

3.   Victims fail to move beyond asking "why" and remain
      _____ in their pain.

      To ask "why" briefly is normal but to stay there is lethal.

THREE REASONS FOR MOVING BEYOND "WHY" TO "WHAT":

1.   Theological reason.

      There are some questions this side of heaven you are never going to
      know.

2.   Emotional reason.

      Anger, guilt and second guessing leads to being emotionally paralyzed.

3.   Pragmatic reason.

      It just doesn't do any good.

The key to moving through your broken world experience is to ask "what" instead of "why".

JAMES, A BOND-SERVANT OF GOD AND OF THE LORD JESUS CHRIST,
TO THE TWELVE TRIBES WHO ARE DISPERSED ABROAD: GREETINGS.
CONSIDER IT ALL JOY, MY BRETHREN, WHEN YOU ENCOUNTER VARIOUS TRIALS,
³KNOWING THAT THE TESTING OF YOUR FAITH PRODUCES ENDURANCE.
⁴AND LET ENDURANCE HAVE ITS PERFECT RESULT, SO THAT YOU MAY
BE PERFECT AND COMPLETE, LACKING IN NOTHING.

JAMES 1:1-4 (NASB)

THREE IMPORTANT QUESTIONS SPIRITUAL CONQUERORS ASK

1.   What can I control?

     Answer: your _____ (v.2)

"EVERYTHING CAN BE TAKEN FROM A MAN BUT ONE THING, THE LAST OF HUMAN FREEDOMS, TO CHOOSE ONE'S ATTITUDE IN ANY GIVEN SET OF CIRCUMSTANCES."

VICTOR FRANKL

You have _____ control of your attitude.

💬 TALK IT OVER

1. What is an area in your life right now that qualifies as a trial?

2. Share a negative experience in your past that (although difficult) has had positive results in your life.

3. Chip said that it is naïve to think life is fair and if you do good and obey God, life will be good to you. How does the Bible paint a different picture of life? Can you think of some verses or passages that speak to this issue?

4. Who is someone that allowed their trials to "make" them instead of "break" them? How did their trial "make" them?

5. Chip said "To ask 'why' briefly is normal but to stay there is lethal. How can it be lethal to stay focused on "why"?

_____

_____

_____

6. There are some questions this side of heaven that are never going to be answered. What question have you been carrying that isn't going to be answered until you get to heaven?

_____

_____

_____

7. What helpful counsel would you give a person who keeps focusing on the fact that they are a "victim"?

_____

_____

_____

☙ LIVE IT OUT

This week spend some time meditating on James 1:1-4. You might want to copy these verses on a card and place them somewhere you will see them every day.

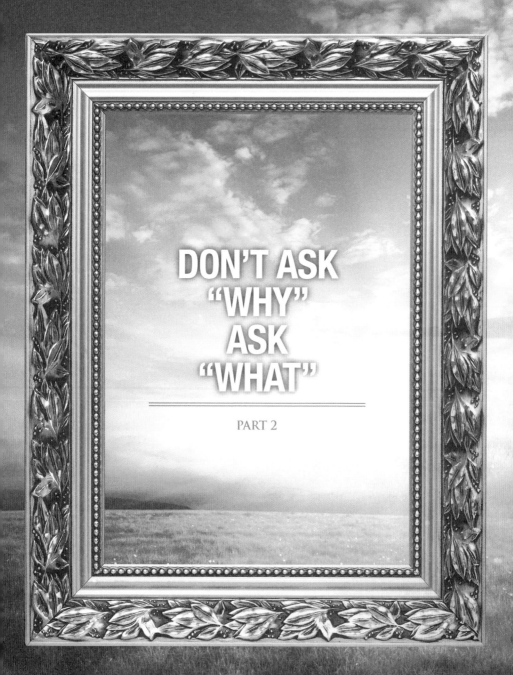

DON'T ASK
"WHY"
ASK
"WHAT"

PART 2

SESSION 2

JOY IS A CHOICE, NOT A FEELING.

> ⁶THEN THE LORD SAID TO CAIN, "WHY ARE YOU ANGRY?
> AND WHY HAS YOUR COUNTENANCE FALLEN?
> ⁷"IF YOU DO WELL, WILL NOT YOUR COUNTENANCE BE LIFTED UP?
>
> GENESIS 4:6-7A (NASB)

SOMETIMES YOU HAVE TO "CHOOSE" YOUR WAY OUT OF A PROBLEM.

THREE IMPORTANT QUESTIONS SPIRITUAL CONQUERORS ASK

1.   What can I control? (From Session 1) James 1:1-4

     Answer: Your attitude (v.2)

2.   What must I do to make it through today?

     Answer: _____ (v.3)

     There is no hypothetical grace. You have grace today and God will give
     you all you need for this moment. When tomorrow comes there will be
     fresh grace.

3. What hope do I have for tomorrow? (v.4)

    Answer: God will take the worst and use it for _____.

    Often the people who reflect Jesus the most are people who have suffered the most.

THE BLESSINGS OF BROKEN-WORLD EXPERIENCES

1. We are forced to _____ on God at a new level.

2   We are _____ from the temporal, the urgent, and the worldly affairs of life.

3. Trials allow us to _____ firsthand the reality and power of God.

4. They serve as an awesome _____ to the unbelieving world.

5. We become sensitive, caring, and compassionate people.

ⓙⓙ TALK IT OVER

1. Describe a time or experience where you had to learn endurance. Share how it impacted you and what you learned.

    _____

    _____

    _____

2. As a group, make a list of some positive byproducts that come from learning endurance.

    _____

    _____

    _____

3. Who are some people in the Bible who learned to endure?

    _____

    _____

    _____

4. Read 2 Corinthians 12:7-10. In what ways did Paul grow and was God glorified by Paul enduring hardship?

    _____

    _____

    _____

5. Read 2 Corinthians 4:16-5:5. What can we learn from this passage about God's purposes for us when life gets hard?

6. Chip said that adversity can help us become more caring and compassionate. How has this truth played itself out in your life?

7. Chip shared 5 ways that God uses adversity to mature us. Which of the 5 statements most speaks to a way that God has worked in your life through trials.

☻ LIVE IT OUT

In this session Chip said the people who reflect Jesus the most are usually the people who have suffered the most. Think of someone you know who has suffered well and allowed their suffering to bring them closer to Jesus. Invite them for coffee or lunch and have them share their story with you.

HELP FOR WHEN YOU'RE "STUCK"

PART 1

SESSION 3

BUT IF ANY OF YOU LACKS WISDOM, LET HIM ASK OF GOD, WHO GIVES TO ALL GENEROUSLY AND WITHOUT REPROACH, AND IT WILL BE GIVEN TO HIM. ⁶BUT HE MUST ASK IN FAITH WITHOUT ANY DOUBTING, FOR THE ONE WHO DOUBTS IS LIKE THE SURF OF THE SEA, DRIVEN AND TOSSED BY THE WIND. ⁷FOR THAT MAN OUGHT NOT TO EXPECT THAT HE WILL RECEIVE ANYTHING FROM THE LORD, ⁸BEING A DOUBLE-MINDED MAN, UNSTABLE IN ALL HIS WAYS.

JAMES 1:5-8 (NASB)

HELP FOR WHEN YOU'RE "STUCK"

1. God's offer is supernatural _____.

    Wisdom = the ability to have the knowledge and understanding and insight to put into practice doing life God's way.

    Wisdom is the _____ to do life God's way.

2. Our responsibility is to _____.

    • _____ is the primary tool in growing through adversity

    • When you are "stuck", the first place to go is _____.

3. God's attitude is generous and without reproach.

    • Generously = lavishly

    • Without reproach = without condemnation

💬 TALK IT OVER

1. One of the reasons some of us don't go to God quickly with our problems is that we have an inaccurate view of God. Our view of God is that he condemns, blames, and punishes. But James says that he responds generously and without reproach (condemnation). When you were young, what was your view of God? How has your understanding of God changed?

2. This session is all about getting practical help when we are "stuck". Describe a time in your life when you faced a problem or trial where you were "stuck".

3. Chip talked about God's offer of wisdom. What is the difference between being smart and being wise? Who is someone you know that exhibits "wisdom"?

4. Our responsibility is to ask God for wisdom. Someone has said that "Prayer should be our first response, not our last resort." When you face a trial, what tends to be your first response?

5. Chip said that "Prayer is the primary tool in growing through adversity." Why is prayer so crucial in helping me grow through times of adversity?

6. Read Matthew 7:7-11. What do these verses teach us about God's disposition toward us? What are the practical implications of these verses for my prayer life?

7. Since prayer is to be our response, spend some time praying for each other and for friends who need God's wisdom.

☻ LIVE IT OUT

This week really focus on going to God first and often. As you encounter problems, trials, and "broken-world experiences", turn to God first. Before you talk to anybody else, talk to God.

HELP FOR WHEN YOU'RE "STUCK"

PART 2

SESSION 4

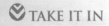

THE LORD IS CLOSE TO THE BROKENHEARTED AND SAVES THOSE WHO ARE CRUSHED IN SPIRIT.

PSALM 34:18 (NIV)

We are never more honest than when we are _____.

OR DO YOU SHOW CONTEMPT FOR THE RICHES OF HIS KINDNESS, TOLERANCE AND PATIENCE, NOT REALIZING THAT GOD'S KINDNESS LEADS YOU TOWARD REPENTANCE?

ROMANS 2:4 (NIV)

BUT WHEN YOU ASK, YOU MUST BELIEVE AND NOT DOUBT, BECAUSE THE ONE WHO DOUBTS IS LIKE A WAVE OF THE SEA, BLOWN AND TOSSED BY THE WIND. 7 THAT PERSON SHOULD NOT EXPECT TO RECEIVE ANYTHING FROM THE LORD.

JAMES 1:6-7 (NIV)

THE ONE CONDITION FOR GOD'S HELP —

"Ask in _____ without any _____."

• What does it mean to "ask in faith"?

Asking in faith is believing or trusting to the point that you have confidence in God's character and God's word to the point of acting on His promises.

The flip side of "faith" is "_____". True belief always leads to obedience.

• What does it mean to have faith "without any doubting"?

Without any doubt means without judgment or wavering.

This is the doubting that has to do with a _____.

Faith without "doubting" involves deciding in advance that we will be obedient to whatever God tells us to do.

FOUR THINGS YOU MUST DO TO GET UNSTUCK

1.   Admit you're stuck.

2.   Admit you can't do it on your own.

3.   Ask God for supernatural wisdom.

4.   Be willing to do _____ God's wisdom demands of you.

⏺ TALK IT OVER

1. When you share when you take risk... If you need wisdom... you tell Him you are willing to do whatever He shows you. Share with the group:

   "Here is where I'm afraid what God might ask me to do". God will give hope, grace and wisdom.

2. When we come broken and honest before God, he will generously give us wisdom. Psalm 34:18 says The LORD is close to the brokenhearted and saves those who are crushed in spirit.

   In your life, how has God responded to you when you have been broken and desperate?

3. Chip said "We are never more honest than when we are desperate." When in your life were you most desperate for God's help?

4. In Romans 2:4 Paul says that God's kindness leads to repentance. How does God's kindness lead to repentance in our lives?

5. Chip used the illustration of a blank check to describe "asking in faith without any doubting". We fill in our name at the bottom before God fills in the top of the check. As a group, make a list of common reasons why we as Christians are fearful to do this?

6. Share an experience from your life where you trusted God and took a step of faith and obedience.

7. Has there ever been a time when you felt God's leading but you resisted or ignored His leading? What happened?

☺ LIVE IT OUT

This week consider taking a blank check and taping it to your bathroom mirror. Every morning this week begin your day by offering the blank check of your obedience. Surrender to God and decide in advance to be obedient to whatever he asks.

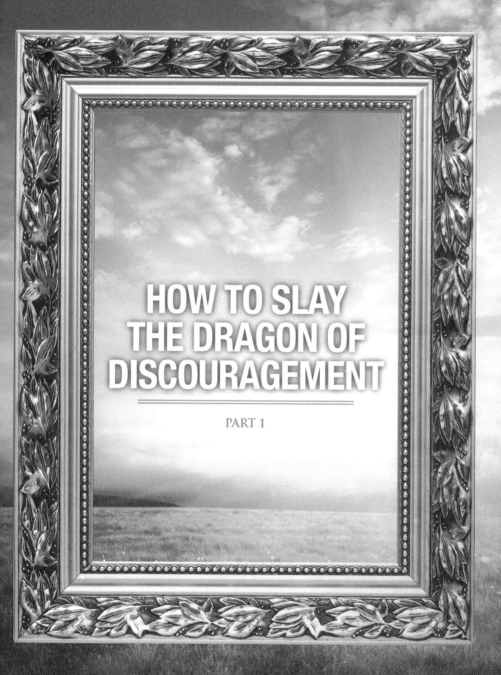

HOW TO SLAY
THE DRAGON OF
DISCOURAGEMENT

PART 1

SESSION 5

Discouragement: 1) to deprive of courage, hope, or confidence; dishearten; 2) to advise or persuade to refrain; 3) prevent or try to prevent by disapproving or raising objections

GOD'S PLAN FOR OVERCOMING DISCOURAGEMENT

1. God's will in adversity is joyful endurance

CONSIDER IT ALL JOY, MY BRETHREN, WHEN YOU ENCOUNTER VARIOUS TRIALS,
³KNOWING THAT THE TESTING OF YOUR FAITH PRODUCES ENDURANCE.
⁴AND LET ENDURANCE HAVE ITS PERFECT RESULT, SO THAT YOU
MAY BE PERFECT AND COMPLETE, LACKING IN NOTHING.

JAMES 1:2-4 (NASB)

2. God's promise in the process is supernatural wisdom

BUT IF ANY OF YOU LACKS WISDOM, LET HIM ASK OF GOD, WHO GIVES TO
ALL GENEROUSLY AND WITHOUT REPROACH, AND IT WILL BE GIVEN TO HIM.
⁶BUT HE MUST ASK IN FAITH WITHOUT ANY DOUBTING, FOR THE ONE WHO
DOUBTS IS LIKE THE SURF OF THE SEA, DRIVEN AND TOSSED BY THE WIND.
⁷FOR THAT MAN OUGHT NOT TO EXPECT THAT
HE WILL RECEIVE ANYTHING FROM THE LORD,
⁸BEING A DOUBLE-MINDED MAN,
UNSTABLE IN ALL HIS WAYS.

JAMES 1:5-8 (NASB)

3. God's prescription for perseverance is divine perspective

> **BUT THE BROTHER OF HUMBLE CIRCUMSTANCES**
> **IS TO GLORY IN HIS HIGH POSITION;**
> **[10]AND THE RICH MAN IS TO GLORY IN HIS HUMILIATION,**
> **BECAUSE LIKE FLOWERING GRASS HE WILL PASS AWAY.**
> **[11]FOR THE SUN RISES WITH A SCORCHING WIND AND WITHERS THE GRASS;**
> **AND ITS FLOWER FALLS OFF AND THE BEAUTY OF ITS APPEARANCE IS DESTROYED;**
> **SO TOO THE RICH MAN IN THE MIDST OF HIS PURSUITS WILL FADE AWAY.**
> **[12]BLESSED IS A MAN WHO PERSEVERES UNDER TRIAL;**
> **FOR ONCE HE HAS BEEN APPROVED, HE WILL RECEIVE THE**
> **CROWN OF LIFE WHICH THE LORD HAS PROMISED**
> **TO THOSE WHO LOVE HIM.**

JAMES 1:9-12 (NASB)

OVERCOMING DISCOURAGEMENT REQUIRES GETTING GOD'S PERSPECTIVE...

1. In our _____ (v.9-11)

    Key: By looking through circumstances through the eyes of faith

2. In our _____ (v.12a)

    Key: By looking at our future through the lens of hope

3. In our _____ (v.12b)

    Key: By looking at our motives through the eyes of love

    Those who have very little materially are forced into a high position spiritually... the position of _____ God.

BECAUSE LIKE FLOWERING GRASS HE WILL PASS AWAY.

JAMES 1:10B (NLT)

TALK IT OVER

1. Describe a time in your life when you were most discouraged. How did you overcome the discouragement?

    _____

    _____

    _____

2. When are you most susceptible to losing perspective and being discouraged?

    _____

    _____

    _____

3. When have you had to trust God the most? What advice would you give someone who is discouraged about learning to trust God?

4. Chip said those who have much materially should place themselves in a low position spiritually... a position of trust and dependency. What would it look like for you to place yourself in a "low position spiritually"?

5. Read Psalm 62:5-8

⁵LET ALL THAT I AM WAIT QUIETLY BEFORE GOD, FOR MY HOPE IS IN HIM.

**⁶HE ALONE IS MY ROCK AND MY SALVATION,
MY FORTRESS WHERE I WILL NOT BE SHAKEN.**

**⁷MY VICTORY AND HONOR COME FROM GOD ALONE.
HE IS MY REFUGE, A ROCK WHERE NO ENEMY CAN REACH ME.**

**⁸O MY PEOPLE, TRUST IN HIM AT ALL TIMES.
POUR OUT YOUR HEART TO HIM, FOR GOD IS OUR REFUGE.**

PSALM 62: 5-8

What hope and truth is there in this passage for those who are discouraged?

6. Spend a few minutes praying together, especially praying for those who might be discouraged. Make "trusting God" the focus of this prayer time.

_____

_____

_____

☺ LIVE IT OUT

This week make it your goal to practice trusting God. Throughout your day... in your prayer time, driving down the road, at meal time, and as you drop into bed at night, let God know that you are trusting him.

HOW TO SLAY THE DRAGON OF DISCOURAGEMENT

PART 2

SESSION 6

**BLESSED IS A MAN WHO PERSEVERES UNDER TRIAL;
FOR ONCE HE HAS BEEN APPROVED, HE WILL RECEIVE THE CROWN
OF LIFE WHICH THE LORD HAS PROMISED TO THOSE WHO LOVE HIM.**

JAMES 1:12 (NASB)

OVERCOMING DISCOURAGEMENT REQUIRES GETTING GOD'S PERSPECTIVE...

1. In our _____ (Covered in Session 5) James 1:9-12

    Key... Looking at circumstances through the eyes of faith.

2. In our _____ (v.12a)

    Key... Looking at our future through the lens of hope.

    • What you are dealing with is not going to last forever.

    • It is a myth that if we really get on track with God He will rearrange all of our circumstances and all of our problems.

    • "the crown of life" = abundant life now and the promise of heaven later.

3. In our _____ (v.12b)

    Key... Looking at our motives through the eyes of love.

Painful and difficult trials provide us the opportunity to express our love to Jesus.

HOW CAN WE SLAY THE DRAGON OF DISCOURAGEMENT?

1. Re-evaluate your circumstances.

    The test: Is my faith in things that are perishable or things that are permanent?

2. Re-evaluate your focus.

    The test: Is my hope determined by the size of my problems or the certainty of God's promises?

3. Re-evaluate your motivation.

    The test: Is the primary motivation of my heart to love Christ or simply get relief?

🗣 TALK IT OVER

1. Chip concluded by talking about 3 ways to overcome discouragement...

    •   Re-evaluate your circumstances
    •   Re-evaluate your focus
    •   Re-evaluate your motivation

    Which of these 3 do you need to work on? How will you do that?

    _____

    _____

    _____

2. Chip talked about looking at life through the lens of eternity rather than just the lens of time. What practical steps could you take to help you have a more eternal perspective in tough times?

    _____

    _____

    _____

3. As a group, come up with a list of practical benefits from having an eternal perspective rather than just a temporal perspective.

    _____

    _____

    _____

4. When you were growing up, what was your view of heaven?

    _____

    _____

    _____

5. Why do you think churches and Christians today don't think and speak about heaven much?

    _____

    _____

    _____

6. Our highest motivation for persevering is love, not duty. What might be some indicators that a persons' relationship with Christ is more about duty than about love?

    _____

    _____

    _____

7. When was your love for Christ most real and intimate? How are you doing these days at deepening your love for Jesus?

    _____

    _____

    _____

❂ LIVE IT OUT

Make this week an "eternity" week, where you look at life through the lens of eternity rather than time. Philippians 3 says that we are "citizens of heaven".

As a way to focus your heart on eternity, every day this week review and meditate on the following verse.

AND WE BELIEVERS ALSO GROAN, EVEN THOUGH WE HAVE
THE HOLY SPIRIT WITHIN US AS A FORETASTE OF FUTURE GLORY,
FOR WE LONG FOR OUR BODIES TO BE RELEASED FROM SIN AND SUFFERING.
WE, TOO, WAIT WITH EAGER HOPE FOR THE DAY WHEN GOD WILL
GIVE US OUR FULL RIGHTS AS HIS ADOPTED CHILDREN,
INCLUDING THE NEW BODIES HE HAS PROMISED US.

ROMANS 8:23

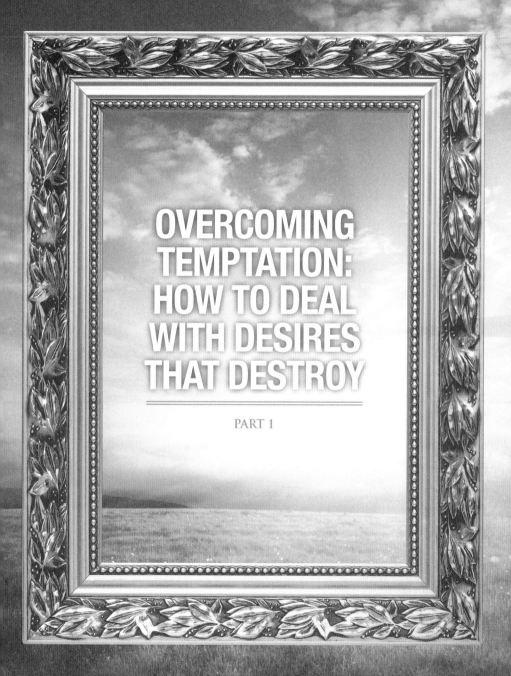

OVERCOMING TEMPTATION: HOW TO DEAL WITH DESIRES THAT DESTROY

PART 1

SESSION 7

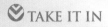

A **trial** is something God wants you to grow through

A **temptation** is something Satan wants you to fall through

Thesis — Under pressure, we are tempted to abandon God's character-building program of endurance and opt for "short cuts" that promise immediate relief, but provide devastating consequences.

How do people fall? _____

LET NO ONE SAY WHEN HE IS TEMPTED, "I AM BEING TEMPTED BY GOD";
FOR GOD CANNOT BE TEMPTED BY EVIL, AND HE HIMSELF DOES NOT TEMPT ANYONE.
¹⁴BUT EACH ONE IS TEMPTED WHEN HE IS CARRIED
AWAY AND ENTICED BY HIS OWN LUST.
¹⁵THEN WHEN LUST HAS CONCEIVED, IT GIVES BIRTH TO SIN;
AND WHEN SIN IS ACCOMPLISHED, IT BRINGS FORTH DEATH.
¹⁶DO NOT BE DECEIVED, MY BELOVED BRETHREN.
¹⁷EVERY GOOD THING GIVEN AND EVERY PERFECT GIFT IS FROM ABOVE,
COMING DOWN FROM THE FATHER OF LIGHTS, WITH WHOM
THERE IS NO VARIATION OR SHIFTING SHADOW.
¹⁸IN THE EXERCISE OF HIS WILL HE BROUGHT US FORTH BY THE WORD OF TRUTH,
SO THAT WE WOULD BE A KIND OF FIRST FRUITS AMONG HIS CREATURES.

JAMES 1:13-18 (NIV)

3 DECEPTIONS THAT WILL DESTROY YOUR LIFE

Deception #1

We are deceived about the _____ of our sin (v. 13-14)

- The Lie – "I'm not responsible for my sin. It's not my fault"

- The Truth – God tempts no one. The problem is not our external circumstances but our internal desires.

- The Application – _____

💬 TALK IT OVER

1. Chip challenged us not to blame or play the "victim", but rather to "own our stuff". Read Psalm 51:1-12 and then discuss what lessons we can learn from David about how to handle our sin. In what way do you tend to go into denial?

2. It's important for us to have an accurate understanding of ourselves. When do you tend to feel most vulnerable to temptation? When you are stressed? Lonely? Discouraged? Tired? Financial pressure?

3. Share a time when you made a bad decision in a time of stress, or loneliness or discouragement.

_____

_____

_____

4. What are some biblical examples of people who were self-deceived?

_____

_____

_____

5. What are some proactive steps that we can take that will protect us from self-deception?

_____

_____

_____

6. John 8:32 (NASB) says you will know the truth, and the truth will make you free. How does "getting real and owning our stuff" set us free?

_____

_____

_____

7. Is there a particular trial you are going through right now? Are you feeling vulnerable to temptation? If you are comfortable doing so, share that with the group and then spend time as a group praying for each other.

❂ LIVE IT OUT

Take Chip's challenge to "get real". Across the top of a 3x5 card write the words Get Real. Then, below prayerfully and honestly fill out the following statement...

I have a problem with....

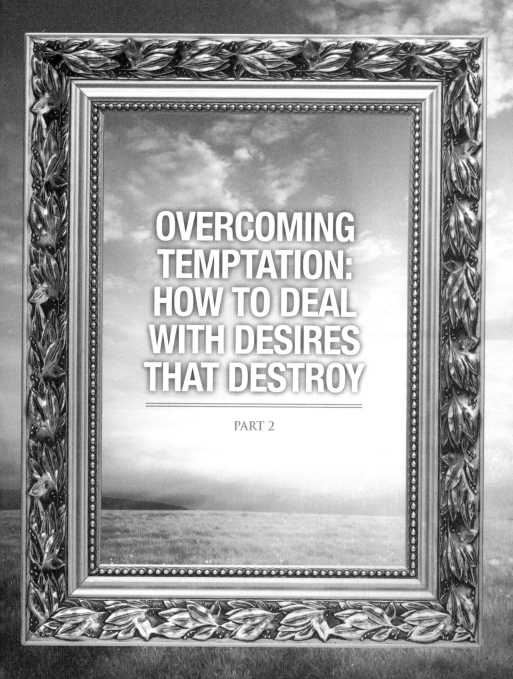

OVERCOMING TEMPTATION: HOW TO DEAL WITH DESIRES THAT DESTROY

PART 2

SESSION 8

3 DECEPTIONS THAT WILL DESTROY YOUR LIFE

Deception #1 (Covered in Session 7) James 1:13-18

We are deceived about the _____ of our sin (v. 13-14)

Deception #2

We are deceived about the _____ of our sin (v.15-16)

- The Lie – "I can handle this. It's not hurting me or anyone else."

- The Truth – Sin is not simply an act; it is the result of a process.

The progression of sin –

Desire > Deception > Design > Disobedience > Death

- Application – _____

Deception #3

We are deceived concerning the nature and _____ of God (v.17-18)

- The Lie – "I've got to party and have my good times now. I'll get serious with God later."

- The Truth – God is good and He will always have my highest and best interest in mind.

> ³²HE WHO DID NOT SPARE HIS OWN SON,
> BUT DELIVERED HIM OVER FOR US ALL,
> HOW WILL HE NOT ALSO WITH HIM
> FREELY GIVE US ALL THINGS?
>
> ROMANS 8:32 (NASB)

GOD'S PROMISE FOR YOU

**NO TEMPTATION HAS OVERTAKEN YOU BUT SUCH
AS IS COMMON TO MAN; AND GOD IS FAITHFUL,
WHO WILL NOT ALLOW YOU TO BE TEMPTED BEYOND
WHAT YOU ARE ABLE, BUT WITH THE TEMPTATION
WILL PROVIDE THE WAY OF ESCAPE ALSO,
SO THAT YOU WILL BE ABLE TO ENDURE IT.**

1 CORINTHIANS 10:13 (NASB)

GOD'S PROVISION FOR ESCAPE INCLUDES

1. Your conscience

2. Scripture (Psalm 119:9-11)

3. Prayer (Matthew 26:41; 6:13)

4. Flight (2 Timothy 2:22)

5. Pre-decisions and planning (Romans 13:14)

💬 TALK IT OVER

1. Sin starts with "desire". That's why it's so important for us to be careful what we put in our mind. For you personally, where do you need to be careful when it comes to your "mental diet"? Are there any changes you need to make in this area?

2. We not only need to be careful about what we put in our mind, but we also need to be careful about following the world's values. Read Romans 12:2 and then share ways that Christians today are tempted to conform to the world. Where do you need to say "no" to the world system?

3. Philippians 4:8 (NASB) says Finally, brethren, whatever is true, whatever is honorable, whatever is right, whatever is pure, whatever is lovely, whatever is of good repute, if there is any excellence and if anything worthy of praise, dwell on these things. What are some practical ways you could begin to put this verse into practice?

4. In the progression of sin, after desire comes deception. Can you think of a time when you were deceived by sin? Share your experience and what you learned?

5. What kind of bait does Satan use to try and snag you?

6. Chip said that "God is good and He will always have my highest and best interest in mind." Even when you have fallen into sin, how have you found this statement to be true in your life?

7. Which of the 5 provisions for escape do you most need to pay attention to?

    •   Conscience

    •   Scripture

    •   Prayer

    •   Flight

    •   Pre-decisions and planning

⊕ LIVE IT OUT

Have a conversation this week with a group friend or family member about the issue of what you put in your mind. Get practical about ways that you can better manage what you put into your mind... and then ask that person to help you monitor this area of your life.

LEADER'S NOTES

GROUP AGREEMENT

People come to groups with a variety of different expectations. The purpose of a group agreement is simply to make sure everyone is on the same page and that we have some common expectations. The following group agreement is a tool to help the group discuss specific guidelines together during your first meeting. Modify anything that does not work for your group, then be sure to discuss the questions that follow. This will help you to have an even greater group experience!

WE AGREE TO THE FOLLOWING PRIORITIES

- Take the Bible Seriously — to seek to understand and apply God's truth in the Bible

- Group Attendance — to give priority to the group meeting (Call if I am going to be absent or late.)

- Safe Environment — to create a safe place where people can be heard and feel loved (no snap judgments or simple fixes)

- Be Confidential — to keep anything that is shared strictly confidential and within the group

- Spiritual Health — to give group members permission to help me live a godly, healthy spiritual life that is pleasing to God

- Building Relationships — to get to know the other members of the group and pray for them regularly

- Prayer — to regularly pray with and for each other

- Other

OUR GAME PLAN

- Will we have refreshments?

  _____

  _____

- What will we do about childcare?

  _____

  _____

- What day and time will we meet?

  _____

  _____

- Where will we meet?

  _____

  _____

- How long will we meet each week?

  _____

  _____

HOW TO MAKE THIS A MEANINGFUL EXPERIENCE FOR YOUR GROUP

BEFORE THE GROUP ARRIVES

1. BE PREPARED. Your personal preparation can make a huge difference in the quality of the group experience. We strongly suggest previewing both the DVD teaching program by Chip Ingram along with the accompanying parts of the study guide.

2. PRAY FOR YOUR GROUP MEMBERS BY NAME. Ask God to use your time together to touch the heart of every person in your group. Expect God to challenge and change people as a result of this study.

3. PROVIDE REFRESHMENTS. There's nothing like food to help a group relax and connect with each other. For the first week, we suggest you prepare a snack, but after that, ask other group members to bring the food so that they share in the responsibilities of the group and make a commitment to return.

4. RELAX. Don't try to imitate someone else's style of leading a group. Lead the group in a way that fits your style and temperament. Remember that people may feel a bit nervous showing up for a small group study, so put them at ease when they arrive. Make sure to have all the details covered prior to your group meeting, so that once people start arriving, you can focus on greeting them.

❤ TAKE IT IN   Watch the Video

1. ARRANGE THE ROOM. Set up the chairs in the room so that everyone can see the television. It's best to arrange the room in such a way that it is conducive to discussion.

2. GET THE VIDEO READY. Each video session on the DVD has 3 components. During the first 2-3 minutes, Chip introduces this week's topic. Then, the group will watch the actual teaching content that Chip taught in front of a live audience. This portion of the video is roughly 25 minutes in length. Finally, Chip will then share some closing thoughts and set up the discussion topics for your group.

3. BE SURE TO TEST YOUR VIDEO EQUIPMENT AHEAD OF TIME. Practice using the equipment and make sure you have located this week's lesson on the DVD menu. The video segments flow from one right into the next. So once you start the session, you won't have to stop the video until Chip has finished his closing thoughts and prepared the group for the first discussion question.

4. HAVE ENOUGH MATERIALS ON HAND. Before you start the video, make sure everyone has their own copy of the study guide. Encourage the group to open to this week's session and follow along with the teaching.

𝟿𝟿 TALK IT OVER

Here are some guidelines for leading the discussion time:

1. MAKE THIS A DISCUSSION, NOT A LECTURE. Resist the temptation to do all the talking and to answer your own questions. Don't be afraid of a few moments of silence while people formulate their answers. And don't feel like you need to have all the answers. There is nothing wrong with simply responding "I don't know the answer to that, but I'll see if I can find an answer this week".

2. ENCOURAGE EVERYONE TO PARTICIPATE. Don't let one person dominate, but also don't pressure quieter members to speak during the first couple of sessions. After one person answers, don't immediately move on; ask what other people think, or say, "Would someone who hasn't shared like to add anything?"

3. AFFIRM PEOPLE'S PARTICIPATION AND INPUT. If an answer is clearly wrong, ask "What led you to that conclusion?" or ask what the rest of the group thinks. If a disagreement arises, don't be too quick to shut it down! The discussion can draw out important perspectives, and if you can't resolve it there, offer to research it further and return to the issue next week. However, if someone goes on the offensive and engages in personal attack of another person, you will need to step in as the leader. In the midst of spirited discussion, we must also remember that people are fragile and there is no place for disrespect.

4. **DETOUR WHEN NECESSARY.** If an important question is raised that is not in the study guide, take time to discuss it. Also, if someone shares something personal and emotional, take time for them. Stop and pray for them right then. Allow the Holy Spirit room to maneuver and follow His prompting when the discussion changes direction.

5. **FORM SUBGROUPS.** One of the principles of small group life is "when numbers go up, sharing goes down". So, if you have a large group, sometimes you may want to split up into groups of 3-5 for discussion time. This is a great way to give everyone, even the quieter members, a chance to say something. Choose someone in the group to guide each of the smaller groups through the discussion. This involves others in the leadership of the group and provides an opportunity for training new leaders.

6. **PRAY.** Be sensitive to the fact that some people in your group may be uncomfortable praying out loud. As a general rule, don't call on people to pray unless you have asked them ahead of time or have heard them pray in public. But this can also be a time to help people build their confidence to pray in a group. Consider having prayer times that ask people to just say a word or sentence of thanks to God.

☉ LIVE IT OUT

These simple suggestions will help you apply the lesson. Be sure and leave adequate time to talk about practical applications of the lesson. This is a great way to build group community.

Try these ideas together and hold each other accountable for completing them, then share the following week how it went.

A FINAL WORD...

Keep an eye on the clock. Be sensitive to time. Whatever is the agreed upon time commitment, try to stick with it. It is always better to finish the meeting with people wanting more rather than people walking away stressed out because the meeting went long.

SESSION NOTES

Thanks for hosting this series called **Rebuilding Your Broken World**. This practical series will help you and your group discover God's plan for handling life's challenges. Whether you are brand new at leading a small group or you are a seasoned veteran, God is going to use you. God has a long history of using ordinary people like us to get his work done.

These brief notes are intended to help prepare you for each week's session. By spending just a few minutes each week previewing the video and going over these leader notes you will set the table for a great group experience. Also, don't forget to pray for your group each week.

Session 1
DON'T ASK "WHY", ASK "WHAT" (1)   7

- If your group doesn't know each other well, be sure that you spend some time getting acquainted. Don't rush right into the video lesson. Remember, small groups are not just about a study or a meeting, they are about relationships.

- Be sure to capture everyone's contact information. It is a good idea to send out an e-mail with everybody's contact information so that the group can stay in touch.

- When you are ready to start the session, be sure that each person in your group has a copy of the study guide. The small group study guide is important for people to follow along and to take notes.

- This series is largely a study through James chapter 1. So, encourage your group to bring their Bibles each week so they can follow along as Chip teaches. If people forget their Bibles, the verses are printed in the study notes.

- The video lesson taught by Chip Ingram will be about 25-30 minutes in length. So, you will have plenty of time for discussion. Each session opens with Chip setting up the lesson. Then, the video will transition to his live teaching. And, at the end of the teaching Chip will come back and wrap up the session as well as set up the first discussion question for the group.

- Facilitating the discussion time. Sometimes Chip will ask you as the facilitator to lead the way by answering the first question. This allows you to lead by example and your willingness to share openly about your life will help others feel the permission to do the same.

- Look over the discussion questions ahead of your group meeting. Since you might not have time to discuss all of them, put a star by the ones you want to be sure and cover.

Session 2
DON'T ASK "WHY", ASK "WHAT" (2)   13

- Why not begin your preparation by praying right now for the people in your group. You might even want to keep their names in your Bible. You may also want to ask people in your group how you can pray for them specifically.

- If somebody doesn't come back this week, be sure and follow up with them. Even if you knew they were going to have to miss the group meeting, give them a call or shoot them an e-mail letting them know that they were missed. It would also be appropriate to have a couple of other people in the group let them know they were missed.

- Each time your group meets take a few minutes to update on what has happened since the last group meeting. Ask people what they are learning and putting into practice. Remember, being a disciple of Jesus means becoming a "doer of the word".

- One of the questions this week asks the group to identify some people in the Bible who learned to endure. You might want to take the lead by sharing about someone like Paul, Job, Joseph, or Moses.

- Live It Out. At the end of the study notes for each session is a section called Live It Out. This section has a couple of ideas or exercises that people in the group could do to deepen their experience with this teaching. Challenge people to really engage these.

Session 3

HELP FOR WHEN YOU'RE "STUCK" (1) 19

- Did anybody miss last week's session? If so, make it a priority to follow up and let them know they were missed. It just might be your care for them that keeps them connected to the group.

- Share the load. One of the ways to raise the sense of ownership within the group is to get them involved in more than coming to the meeting. So, get someone to help with refreshments... find somebody else to be in charge of the prayer requests... get someone else to be in charge of any social gathering you plan... let someone else lead the discussion one night. Give away as much of the responsibility as possible. That is GOOD leadership.

- Think about last week's meeting for a moment. Was there anyone that didn't talk or participate? In every group there are extroverts and there are introverts. There are people who like to talk and then there are those who are quite content NOT to talk. Not everyone engages in the same way or at the same level but you do want to try and create an environment where everyone wants to participate.

- Follow up questions. The only thing better than good questions are good follow up questions. Questions are like onions. Each question allows another layer to be peeled back and get beneath the surface.

- Don't be afraid of silence. When you ask people a question, give them time to think about it. Don't feel like you have to fill every quiet moment with words.

- Part of this week's session focuses on prayer. Your group will be encouraged to spend some time praying for each other at the end of the session. Be sure to leave enough time that the group doesn't feel rushed in praying for each other.

Session 4

- As you get the group together this week, do a check in from last week. Ask people if they did the Live It Out exercise. They were challenged to go to God first and often with their problems. Don't shame or embarrass people if they didn't do it, but encourage them to do it this coming week.

- Don't feel any pressure to get through all the questions. As people open up and talk, don't move on too quickly. Give them the space to share what is going on inside them as they interact with this teaching.

- If your group is not sharing as much as you would like or if the discussion is being dominated by a person or two, try subgrouping. If your group is 8 people or more, this is a great way to up the level of participation. After watching the DVD, divide the group into a couple of smaller groups for the discussion time. It is good to get someone you think would be a good facilitator to agree to this ahead of time.

- One of the questions this week asks "when in your life were you most desperate for God's help?" This could be a threatening question for some people in your group. Let people share at whatever level they are comfortable and don't call on anyone to answer this question. Let them share voluntarily.

- Encourage the whole group this week to do the Live It Out challenge. The group will be asked to take a blank check and tape it to their bathroom mirror. As they start their day, it is a symbol and reminder of our surrender to God.

Session 5

- You are now at the halfway point of this series. How is it going? How well is the group connecting? What has been going well and what needs a little work? Are there any adjustments you need to make?

- Confidentiality is crucial to group life. The moment trust is breached, people will shut down and close up. So, you may want to mention the importance of confidentiality again this week just to keep it on people's radar.

- This week's session is about discouragement. As people talk about their struggles with discouragement, practice the ministry of "presence". Sometimes, there aren't quick fixes or simple answers to the deep problems people face. Perhaps the greatest gift you offer is not what you say, but your friendship, care, and support.

- Be sensitive to someone who is right now in a season of discouragement and depression. Don't be afraid to stop the discussion for a few minutes and have the group gather around and pray for that person.

Session 6

HOW TO SLAY THE DRAGON OF DISCOURAGEMENT (2) 39

- One way to deepen the level of community within your group is to spend time together outside the group meeting. If you have not already done so, plan something that will allow you to get to know each other better. Also, consider having someone else in the group take responsibility for your fellowship event.

- As you begin this week's session, do a check-in to see what people are learning and applying from this series. Don't be afraid to take some time at the beginning of your meeting to review some key ideas from the previous week's lessons.

- Consider asking someone in your group to facilitate next week's lesson. Who knows, there might be a great potential small group leader in your group. It will give you a break and give them a chance to grow.

- This week's Live It Out challenge is to meditate on Romans 8:23. You might want to consider passing out 3x5 cards to everyone in the group and having them write out the verse. Then challenge them to review it and reflect on it several times this week.

OVERCOMING TEMPTATION: HOW TO DEAL WITH DESIRES THAT DESTROY (1)   45

- Since this is the next to the last week of this study, you might want to spend some time this week talking about what your group is going to do after your complete this study.

- As this series winds down, this is a good time to plan some kind of party or fellowship after you complete the study. Find the "party person" in your group and ask them to take on the responsibility of planning a fun experience for the group. Also, use this party as a time for people to share how God has used this series to grow them and change them.

- During this session, the group will be asked to identify some people in the Bible who were self-deceived. To get the discussion going, you might take the lead and share about David when he committed adultery with Bathsheba or the Pharisees (Matthew 23)

- The last discussion question will ask people if there is a particular trial or temptation they are facing right now. If they are comfortable doing so, they are asked to share that struggle with the group. Be sure to highlight the importance of confidentiality and that the group is to be a "safe place".

- The Live It Out challenge this week requires a 3x5 card. You might want to provide those for the group. Each group member will be asked to write across the top of the card the words "I Have a Problem With...". Then they honestly write down the issue they are struggling with. It would be good for you to encourage them to share their card this week with a trusted friend.

Session 8

OVERCOMING TEMPTATION: HOW TO DEAL WITH DESIRES THAT DESTROY (2)   51

- Since this is your last session in this series, make sure that you have talked about what your group is going to do next. Also, consider taking a week or two break and doing a party/fellowship together. For some additional options for small group curriculum look at livingontheedge.org.

- Spend a few minutes prior to your meeting praying for your group. This final session is all about sin's destructive potential and how we can overcome it. This session has the potential to raise some deep and painful issues. So, come to this session prayed up!

- As you close out this session you might want to take a few minutes and reflect on the entire series. Ask the group members to share the most significant lesson they have learned from this series.

PRAYER AND PRAISE

One of the most important things you can do in your group is to pray with and for each other. Write down each other's concerns here so you can remember to pray for these requests during the week!

Use the Follow Up box to record an answer to a prayer or to write down how you might want to follow up with the person making the request. This could be a phone call, an e-mail, or a card. Your personal concern will mean a lot!

PERSON	PRAYER REQUEST	FOLLOW UP

PERSON	PRAYER REQUEST	FOLLOW UP

PERSON	PRAYER REQUEST	FOLLOW UP

PERSON	PRAYER REQUEST	FOLLOW UP

PERSON	PRAYER REQUEST	FOLLOW UP

PERSON	PRAYER REQUEST	FOLLOW UP

GROUP ROSTER

NAME	HOME PHONE	EMAIL

WHAT'S NEXT?

More Group Studies from Chip Ingram

NEW BIO
Quench Your Thirst for Life

5 video sessions

Cinematic story illustrates Biblical truth in this 5-part video study that unlocks the Biblical DNA for spiritual momentum by examining the questions at the heart of true spirituality.

NEW House or Home Marriage
God's Blueprint for a Great Marriage

10 video sessions

The foundational building blocks of marriage are crumbling before our eyes, and Christians aren't exempt. It's time to go back to the blueprint and examine God's plan for marriages that last for a lifetime.

NEW Good to Great in God's Eyes
10 Practices Great Christians Have in Common

10 video sessions

If you long for spiritual breakthrough, take a closer look at ten powerful practices that will rekindle a fresh infusion of faith and take you from good to great...in God's eyes.

Balancing Life's Demands
Biblical Priorities for Busy Lives

10 video sessions

Busy, tired and stressed out? Learn how to put "first things first" and find peace in the midst of pressure and adversity.

Effective Parenting in a Defective World
Raising Kids that Stand Out from the Crowd

9 video sessions

Packed with examples and advice for raising kids, this series presents Biblical principles for parenting that still work today.

Experiencing God's Dream for Your Marriage
Practical Tools for a Thriving Marriage

12 video sessions

Examine God's design for marriage and the real life tools and practices that will transform it for a lifetime.

Watch previews & order at www.LivingontheEdge.org

Five Lies that Ruin Relationships
Building Truth-Based Relationships

10 video sessions

Uncover five powerful lies that wreck relationships and experience the freedom of understanding how to recognize God's truth.

The Genius of Generosity
Lessons from a Secret Pact Between Friends

4 video sessions

The smartest financial move you can make is to invest in God's Kingdom. Learn His design for wise giving and generous living.

God As He Longs for You To See Him
Getting a Right View of God

10 video sessions

A deeper look at seven attributes of God's character that will change the way you think, pray and live.

Holy Ambition
Turning God-Shaped Dreams Into Reality

7 video sessions

Do you long to turn a God-inspired dream into reality? Learn how God uses everyday believers to accomplish extraordinary things.

Invisible War
The Believer's Guide to Satan, Demons & Spiritual Warfare

8 video sessions

Are you "battle ready"? Learn how to clothe yourself with God's "spiritual armor" and be confident of victory over the enemy of your soul.

Living On The Edge
Becoming a Romans 12 Christian

10 video sessions

If God exists...what does he want from us? Discover the profile of a healthy disciple and learn how to experience God's grace.

Love, Sex & Lasting Relationships
God's Prescription to Enhance Your Love Life
10 video sessions

Do you believe in "true love"? Discover a better way to find love, stay in love, and build intimacy that lasts a lifetime.

The Miracle of Life Change
How to Change for Good
10 video sessions

Ready to make a change? Explore God's process of true transformation and learn to spot barriers that hold you back from receiving God's best.

Overcoming Emotions that Destroy
Constructive Tools for Destructive Emotions
10 video sessions

We all struggle with destructive emotions that can ruin relationships. Learn God's plan to overcome angry feelings for good.

Rebuilding Your Broken World
How God Puts Broken Lives Back Together
8 video sessions

Starting over? Learn how God can reshape your response to trials and bring healing to broken relationships and difficult circumstances.

Why I Believe
Answers to Life's Most Difficult Questions
12 video sessions

Examine the Biblical truth behind the pivotal questions at the heart of human existence and the claims of the Christian faith.

Your Divine Design
Discover, Develop and Deploy Your Spiritual Gifts
8 video sessions

How has God uniquely wired you? Discover God's purpose for spiritual gifts and how to identify your own.